Weekly Reader Children's Book Club presents

PHOEBE
and
THE GENERAL

SAMUEL FRAUNCES

JUDITH BERRY GRIFFIN
PHOEBE
and
THE GENERAL
ILLUSTRATED BY
MARGOT TOMES

Coward, McCann & Geoghegan, Inc.   New York

Text copyright © 1977 *by Judith Berry Griffin*
Illustrations copyright © 1977 *by Margot Tomes*

Published simultaneously in
Canada by Longman Canada Limited, Toronto.
SBN: GB-698-30629-5
SBN: TR-698-20377-1
PRINTED IN THE UNITED STATES OF AMERICA

Library of Congress Cataloging in Publication Data
Griffin, Judith Berry.
  Phoebe and the general.
  SUMMARY: During the Revolution, Phoebe Fraunces
has a chance to save the life of General George
Washington while he has dinner at Mortier
House in New York City.
  1.   Washington, George, Pres. U. S., 1732-1799—
Juvenile literature. 2.   Fraunces, Phoebe—Juve-
nile literature. [1.   Washington, George, Pres.
U. S., 1732-1799. 2.   Fraunces, Phoebe] I.   Tomes,
Margot. II.   Title.
E312.17.G74   1976   973.4'1'0924   [B]   76-8921

To Jean Fritz

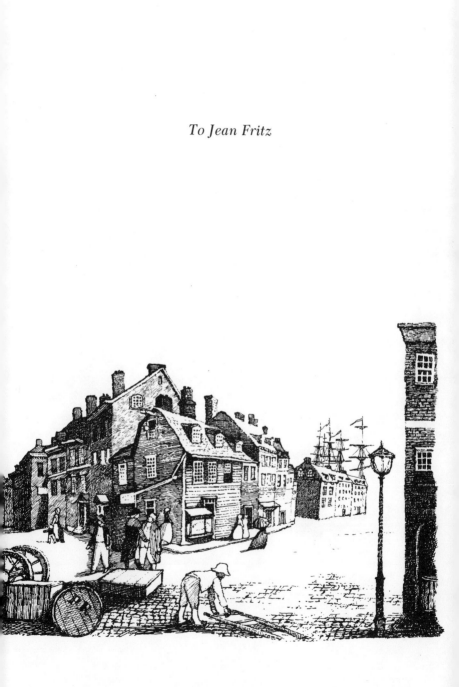

In 1776, the year Phoebe Fraunces was thirteen years old, her father gave her a very dangerous job. Phoebe was going to be a spy.

At that time most black people in New York were slaves. But Phoebe and her family had always been free. Phoebe's father, Samuel Fraunces, owned the Queen's Head Tavern. The Queen's Head was a popular eating and meeting place. George Washington (who was now General George Washington, commander in chief of the American Army) had dinner there when he visited New York. So did John Adams.

Many people met there because they knew it was a safe place to talk. In 1776 the war had begun, and there could be trouble if a person were caught talking against the king. But the Patriots knew that Samuel Fraunces could be trusted. So they held meetings at his tavern and discussed their secret plans, and Sam Fraunces never let on that he knew any of them.

One morning in April, 1776, Sam and his daughter Phoebe were sitting side by side in the long dining room of the Queen's Head. There was to be a big dinner that night, and they were getting the room ready—polishing the pewter plates and candlesticks and laying out fresh candles.

Phoebe loved the Queen's Head from its broad front steps all the way up to its bright red-tiled roof. But this room—called the Long Room—was the room she loved best, with its neat tables and chairs, its fireplaces and its big windows. From the window seat where she sat she could see clear to the harbor. The water was dotted with big white-sailed ships, their tall masts pointing at the sky like fingers.

"Phoebe," her father began.

"Yes, sir," Phoebe answered. Her father did not re-

spond, and Phoebe looked up at him, smiling. She thought him very handsome, with his curly hair powdered and drawn back and his smooth brown skin and dark eyes.

"Phoebe, I've something important to say to you this day," he said. "It's a bad time in this country."

Phoebe stopped smiling when she saw he was so serious.

"It's hard to find a person you can trust with a secret— especially a dangerous secret," he went on. "I'm glad to know I can trust you. Young as you are, you've learned from your father how to listen well and talk little."

Something in her father's voice made Phoebe put down the candlestick she was holding. She sat quite still, waiting for him to go on, watching the polishing cloth in his hands go around and around.

"I have a great fear in me," he said slowly, "that our

9

General Washington is in dread, dread danger. It is he who is keeping the colonies together. But there are those who'd like to see the colonies separated and so ruled more easily by the king. And if something were to happen to the general, it would be a hard, hard job to find another such as he, to pull the colonies together and throw off the king. Indeed, such a man might not be found at all, and the king would rule on."

There was silence for a time. The sunlight, stronger now, pushed warm fingers through the windows, glittering against the candlesticks.

"New York is full of soldiers," he continued. "Some are only out for money. To them it makes no difference what side they're on. They'd even take money from the enemy and do anything they'd ask. Some such scoundrel might be paid to kill the general. I heard something."

Phoebe closed her eyes, seeing her father moving like a shadow among his guests, gracious, smiling, pouring wine and exchanging greetings. It was so easy for him to hear secrets without seeming to listen!

"What I heard could cost my life, Daughter, and the general's as well," her father said quietly. "Phoebe, I need your help."

Phoebe opened her mouth to speak, but her voice would only whisper. "What must I do?" she asked.

Her father put down the candlestick and took her hand in his. "I want you to do a big job, Phoebe," he said gravely. "General Washington has let me know he's arriving in New York with his household in seven days' time. He's to move into Mortier House on Richmond Hill, and I promised to find him a housekeeper. I want you to live there and be his housekeeper, Phoebe. I know you will be a good one. But your real job will be to watch—to listen—to spy out every bit of information you can. I want you to find out if there is someone planning to kill him and how he plans to do it. Your real job will be to save General Washington's life."

Phoebe was very frightened. General Washington was a great soldier! How could she save his life, if his whole army could not? She wouldn't know who to look for. She was not even strong enough to fight anyone! And what if she failed?

Her father spoke again, as if he had read her thoughts. "I'm asking only that you try, Daughter," he said. "I have no proof of a plot against the general's life. I know only what I heard. If I tell, his enemies would only hide themselves and wait for a safer time."

Phoebe shook her head. Could this really be happening? But her father's voice was real. "You'll tell no one who you are. You'll listen as you serve the officers of the Army. You

12

must watch for a member of General Washington's body-guard—someone whose name begins with T. It is this man who is supposed to carry out the plan. Every day you and I will meet down by the market, and you can tell me what news you have.

"Now hear me well, Phoebe. You are to do nothing by yourself —nothing that would put you in danger. You are only to listen and tell me what you hear. Trust no one. No one." He picked up his candlestick and began to polish it once more. When he spoke this time, his voice sounded sad, but Phoebe heard more than sadness. Her father was angry.

"You know, Phoebe," he said, " 'tis a strange freedom we're fighting for, alongside George Washington."

Phoebe nodded. She knew what her father meant. How could a man lead an army to win freedom if he himself owned slaves? For General Washington did own slaves. It was said he treated them well. But still, they were slaves.

IN PORT at
CHARLESTON
The *Brigantine* BETSY
JOSIAH WILLARD, *Master*

Carrying able-bodied AFRICAN
Both **MALE & FEMALE**
Interested Persons should make
Inquiries at Wharf
* * * * * *

For **WEST INDIA**
Departing on the **TUES.** *Instant R.*

"And 'tis stranger yet that you and I will save him," Samuel went on. "And those like us will have no share in that freedom he's fighting for!"

"But maybe," Phoebe said, "when the Patriots win their freedom, they'll let the slaves go free, too. Maybe then everyone will be free!"

Samuel shook his head. "I think not, Daughter," he said. "But maybe, one day. . . ." Then he looked at Phoebe and smiled. "Here, now! Get on with your polishing! It won't do to have tonight's dinner set off by dull candlesticks!"

And so it was that a few days later Phoebe packed two clean aprons and a bottle of her father's best cider into a bundle, said good-bye to her family, and set off to save George Washington's life.

Mortier House was just a few blocks from the Queen's Head, but Phoebe felt as if she were going miles and miles away from home as she slowly made her way through the narrow, winding, crowded streets. A cold, damp wind blew in off the harbor. Everywhere, it seemed, men were pushing carts. They rattled over the cobblestones, loaded with guns and ammunition. Soldiers were everywhere, shouting orders. War was in the air.

Mortier House sat high on a hill, with a carpet of grass around it that reached away to the large, beautiful trees beyond. There was a small storage house to one side, with a hen house and yard where several chickens pecked and scratched contentedly. Phoebe followed the long drive to the back of the house, wondering how soon she would meet someone whose name began with T and what she would do when she did. Mortier House was quiet and calm, quite a change from the busy street, but here, too, war was in the air.

A tall, thin woman opened the back door. She looked very surprised when Phoebe told her who she was. "Why, you're nothin' but a child!" she said. "How are you going to take care of this big place?"

"I'm strong," replied Phoebe, standing as tall as she could. "And I work hard. I'll have no trouble."

The woman looked at her doubtfully. "Well," she said, "leastways you talk right up. I'm Mary. I cook. This here's Pompey," she continued as a boy about eight appeared from behind her. "He's my boy. He'll be a help to you— bringing in firewood and such like that."

She led Phoebe through room after room of beautiful, shining furniture, up stairs and more stairs, across carpeted floors—all silent and waiting. Finally, on the top floor of

the house, they stopped before a door that Mary opened into a tiny room. It contained a small window and a narrow cot. "This is yours," she said. "I'm in the kitchen should you need me."

As soon as the door closed, Phoebe sank down on the cot. Already she missed the Queen's Head and her father. If she were home now, she'd be helping him ready the tables for dinner. At the thought of her father Phoebe rocked back and forth on the cot in despair, still clutching her bundle. How could she take care of this big, quiet, unfriendly house, with its gleaming floors and stiff furniture? And take care of General Washington, too? She could not do it. Her father had asked too much.

After a while she stood up and walked toward the window. She could see out over much of the city. Over there was the fort. Here were the harbor and the tall spire of Trinity Church. And could it be—she looked harder—yes, it was! There, among all the dark-brown and black roofs of the other buildings, was the bright red-tiled roof of the Queen's Head! It stood out like a flag, almost like a signal! And suddenly, Phoebe did not feel so hopeless. She wasn't so far from home, after all. She would see her father every day. And she was to do nothing by herself—he had said so. His words came back to her: "I only want you to try, Daughter." Phoebe sighed and began to untie her bundle.

Phoebe soon settled into her job. The work wasn't as hard as she thought it would be. Mrs. Washington had brought her own quilts and feather beds. It was Phoebe's job to air and turn these every morning, as well as to see to the buying of food and the serving of meals. She had to keep the silver cleaned and shining and the furniture dusted and polished. She did not have any special jobs to do for General Washington, except to see that his meals were served on time. He was very particular about having dinner served promptly at four o'clock, and Phoebe sometimes had a hard time getting everything finished by then.

General Washington never said very much. He was tall, with a quiet voice. He looked like the kind of man who could win a war. Mrs. Washington was to have a fresh egg each day, and Pompey, who was a lot of company to Phoebe even though he was only eight years old, helped by visiting the hen house early every morning. When dinner was over, he and Phoebe often stood on the kitchen steps and fed the hens leftover scraps of bread from the table.

Phoebe was a good housekeeper. But she did not forget why she was there. Day after day she watched, and waited, and listened. General Washington came and went. The house was full of people all the time—officers of the Army, friends, members of the bodyguard. Phoebe slipped among them silent as a shadow, as her father had taught her. Whenever she saw anyone talking softly, she stopped to poke the fire, fill their glasses, light new candles. But still she saw nothing, heard nothing.

Each day at noon she took a basket and went down to the waterfront to do the day's marketing. When she was finished, she would make her way to the edge of the harbor and stand looking out over the ocean. No one took any notice of her, in her clean white apron and cap, a shawl thrown across her shoulders. Nor did anyone particularly notice the man who always came to stand beside her, his curly hair powdered and pulled back, his brown face plump and smiling.

The two of them would stand together for a few moments, seeming to talk of nothing important. Sometimes Phoebe would throw out a few crumbs to the gulls, which would gather noisily at their feet. After a time they would move off in different directions—Phoebe back to Mortier House, Sam Fraunces back to the Queen's Head.

Phoebe never had anything to report. She was particularly careful to watch every member of the general's bodyguard who came to the house. None was called by a name starting with T. They all seemed to be truly fond of the general and laughed and joked with him. Two members of the bodyguard did stand out from the others. One was especially nice. Mr. Hickey was his name. He smiled at Phoebe while she was serving and often came into the kitchen to joke with her and Mary while Mary was preparing the meals.

Phoebe was the youngest servant in the house except for Pompey. When the others were talking, she often felt left out. She was glad to have someone to talk to. Hickey seemed much younger than the other men—not much older, in fact, than Phoebe herself. And he seemed glad to talk to her, too. Like Phoebe, he seemed not to have many friends. Phoebe often saw him sitting by himself at the edge of the woods.

Mr. Green was another member of General Washington's bodyguard who kept to himself, but he was not like Hickey. He never spoke to Phoebe at all, even when he saw her in the yard. Phoebe would always say, "Evening, sir," but he never so much as looked at her. From what she could tell, he didn't say much to anyone, even at dinnertime when everyone did a lot of talking. Though his name didn't begin with T, Phoebe made up her mind to watch him very carefully. There was something about him she didn't like.

One day, when Hickey came to the kitchen, he had a small cloth bag with him. He handed it to Phoebe. "Here," he said. "It's some seed for your precious chickens."

Phoebe was surprised. She didn't know anyone had noticed that she fed them. She opened the bag. "But it's good seed, sir!" she protested. "It's too good to feed the chickens!"

Hickey laughed. "It's only the king's true men who'll be missing it," he said. "Let's see if your chickens will get fatter from British grain than from American bread crumbs!"

Phoebe smiled. She didn't ask him how he had got the seed. But he began to bring it home to her often. Sometimes he would bring it himself. Other times she would find a bag lying on the table when she came into the kitchen. Sometimes there would be a bright ribbon tied around it. Then Hickey would say, "The ribbon's for you, pretty Phoebe. Compliments of King George III!" Sometimes there would be a stick of candy inside—always, he said, stolen from those loyal to the King of England.

Soon she was looking forward to his visits every day. And as the days went by and Phoebe still could find no one who seemed to be plotting to take General Washington's life, she thought about asking Mr. Hickey for help. Her father had told her to trust no one. Still . . . perhaps she could trust him. She would wait and see.

Weeks went by. The beautiful house, once so strange to her, was now like a good friend. Phoebe enjoyed using the fine china plates and crystal glasses. She enjoyed serving Mary's deliciously prepared meals to General Washington and his important guests, while Pompey followed solemnly behind with the salt cellar and pepper mill.

She knew she was there to save General Washington's life. But as the days went by and she still heard nothing, she began to wonder if perhaps her father was mistaken. No one seemed to be plotting anything, and it was now the beginning of June. Phoebe had been at Mortier House almost two months.

Then one day, when she went to the market, her father wasn't there. Phoebe stood by the water a long time, waiting and wondering. Should she go to the Queen's Head? Or back to Mortier House? As she was trying to decide, she saw her father hurrying toward her. He looked very worried. For the first time he seemed not to care that people might notice them. He held her by the shoulders and looked into her face.

"Phoebe," he said urgently, "I have heard that General Washington will be leaving Mortier House in a very few days. The person known as T will act before that time. You must find out who it is!"

Phoebe's mind was whirling as she hurried back toward the house. She was frightened, but she was also determined. She *would* save General Washington! She had long ago figured that he would likely be shot. During dinner he always sat in a chair by the window. He would make an easy target for anyone waiting outside.

If only she could get him to change his place, away from that window! His good friend General Gates would be a dinner guest at the house this evening. Everyone else was part of the family or a member of the bodyguard. Over and over she said their names. No one's name began with T.

As she reached the kitchen door, she saw Hickey sitting on the steps. "Why are you so solemn, pretty Phoebe?" he asked.

"Oh, Mr. Hickey, sir," said Phoebe breathlessly. "I'm so worried. . . ." She paused. She did need help! Should she tell him? Maybe he knew something, had seen something that had escaped her notice. After all, he was a member of the bodyguard—it was his job to protect General Washington. Her father's words came back to her. "Trust no one," he had said. "No one." She sighed. She'd have to keep trying alone.

"Well," said Hickey after a moment. "I've something to bring a smile back to that pretty face. Fresh June peas for the general's dinner—first of the season! His favorite and mine—and enough for us both! Some friends of the king will be mighty hungry tonight!" He handed her a large sack, filled to the brim with pea pods. Phoebe smiled in spite of herself.

"Grown men—soldiers of the American Army—stealing peas!" she said.

Hickey pretended to be hurt. "All right," he said, snatching the sack from her and holding it over his head. "I'll just throw them out to your chickens—"

"No, no, Mr. Hickey." Phoebe laughed. "Here—I'll fix them myself."

Hickey handed her the sack. "I'll be here to fill my plate at dinnertime," he promised.

All afternoon, as she went about her chores, Phoebe worried. *How* could she get the general's chair away from that window? She would have to stand in front of it, blocking the view from outside. But then, would someone shoot her? By the time dinnertime arrived she was almost sick with fear. She was in the kitchen with Pompey getting ready to serve the plates when a voice behind her made her jump. It was Hickey.

"I've come for my peas," he said softly.

"Oh! Mr. Hickey, sir!" she said. "You gave me such a start! I was—" She stopped and looked at him, even more startled. He looked ill? frightened? She couldn't tell which.

"Which is my plate, and which is General Washington's?" he said. "It wouldn't do for him to have more than me." He spoke quickly, without smiling this time.

"I never heard of such carryings on over a pile of peas!" Phoebe said. "This is the general's plate, and this is yours!"

She turned away to fill Pompey's salt cellar and turned back just in time to see Hickey's hand move quickly away from General Washington's plate and slide into his pocket. Something winked for a second in the light—something shiny, like glass.

"What are you doing to General Washington's plate?" she said. "I told you yours is here!" She picked up the plate. Was it her imagination, or was there something grainy, like sugar, on the peas? Phoebe looked more closely, but as she looked, whatever it was seemed to have disappeared. An instant later she wasn't sure—had she seen anything at all? She thought of the window again and forgot about the peas. She had to serve General Washington.

Leaving Hickey standing in the kitchen, Phoebe nervously entered the dining room, Pompey following with the salt. As she walked toward the general, Phoebe looked at every face around the table. Some of the guests were talking, some merely smiling. None seemed nervous or frightened.

And then she noticed the empty chair. Who was missing? But even as she asked herself the question, she knew. It was Mr. Green. Was he outside the house, with a gun, waiting? General Washington was sitting by the window, as she had feared. He sat back easily in his chair, listening to something General Gates was saying. The window was open! As she went past, Phoebe looked outside anxiously. There was not a sound, not a shadow, not a movement. The green grass was smooth and unruffled. Even the leaves in the trees beyond were still.

"Well, Phoebe!" General Washington exclaimed as she stopped beside his chair. "June peas! How did you get them so early in the season?"

"It wasn't me, sir," replied Phoebe, looking past him out the window. "It was your Mr. Hickey brought them in, fresh today. He says they're your favorite."

"And mine as well!" said General Gates. "Where is Mr. Thomas Hickey? I want to thank him!"

Phoebe started to put the plate down in front of General Washington. Then, in a flash, it came to her who she was looking for. Mr. Green was not hiding outside the window to shoot at the general. The person who was trying to kill him was here—in the kitchen! Phoebe stood like a stone, the plate still in her hands. She saw Hickey again—Thomas Hickey—laughing and teasing, bringing her candy and ribbons and seed for her chickens. And then bringing June peas for the general and sprinkling them with poison! T was for Thomas, member of General Washington's bodyguard!

Still holding the plate, she whirled around. Pompey was waiting behind her. "Run!" she screamed. "Run! Get my father!"

Everyone stopped talking. Pompey looked at her in amazement. "Y-your father?" he stammered.

"Sam Fraunces! At the Queen's Head! Go!" And she stamped her foot. Pompey had never heard Phoebe sound like that before. He dropped the salt cellar and ran through the kitchen door.

Everyone in the dining room sat frozen. All eyes were on Phoebe. "General Washington!" she cried. "Mr. Hickey has put poison in your dinner! I saw him!" There was a gasp from the table.

"What jest is this?" roared General Gates, getting up from his place and reaching for the plate. But before he could take it from her, Phoebe ran to the open window and threw the whole plate out into the yard.

Now the dining room was in an uproar. Chairs overturned; wine spilled as the men jumped to their feet in confusion. Some ran toward the window where Phoebe was standing, as if they feared she might try to escape. Others started for the kitchen. Some ran to surround General Washington. No one knew what to do.

It was General Gates who first noticed the chickens in the yard. "By God!" he shouted, pointing out the window. "Look!"

Three of Phoebe's chickens had come to peck at the peas she had thrown outside. Two had already fallen dead. The third was still moving its wings, but as they watched, it, too, grew still. The poison, meant for General Washington, had killed the chickens instead.

"Get Hickey!" bellowed General Gates, and members of the bodyguard rushed to obey. Minutes later Thomas Hickey was dragged in from the yard, his face white with terror. He had not been able to escape. Minutes after that, Sam Fraunces burst into the room. Phoebe was still standing by the window, shaking. He ran to her and held her tightly. Phoebe clung to him, burying her face in his shoulder.

"Well done, Daughter," Samuel Fraunces said quietly. "Well done."

After the excitement had died down and Hickey had been taken away, General Washington came to speak to Phoebe and her father. "It's nice to know people whom I can trust," he said simply. "Thank you."

General Washington went on to lead the American Army to victory, and the United States was born. So freedom did come to some Americans, but not all. In 1783, when the war was won, General Washington chose to give his victory party at Fraunces' Queen's Head Tavern, and there he said good-bye to the leaders of his army. And when he became the first President of the United States, he invited Sam Fraunces to become his official steward. Fraunces held that job until 1796.

Thomas Hickey was tried and convicted of trying to kill George Washington. Seven days later he was hanged. As was usual in those days, everyone turned out to watch. No one knows whether Phoebe was there. No one knows what happened to Phoebe after that. But we do know that she was a good spy.

Thank you, Phoebe Fraunces.

Postscript from the Author

The story of Phoebe Fraunces is essentially historically accurate. Samuel Fraunces did indeed allow his restaurant to serve as a meeting place for the Patriots. He was so steadfast in his loyalty to the revolutionary cause that after the war ended he was voted the sum of £200 by Congress, as a reward. Soon after that Fraunces changed the name of the Queen's Head to the name by which it is still known today—Fraunces Tavern. The tavern is still standing, at the corner of Broad and Pearl streets in New York City. Part of it is a museum, but the bottom floor still operates as a restaurant. It looks very much as it did when Samuel Fraunces and his family lived there, except that it no longer has its red-tiled roof.